The Woman Who Invented Weaving
Copyright © 2019 by Christopher Davis, Jr.

All rights reserved. This book or any portion thereof
may not be reproduced or used in any manner whatsoever
without the express written permission of the author
except for the use of brief quotations in a book review.

Printed in the United States of America

First Printing, 2019

ISBN 978-0-578-43937-2

Author Christopher Davis, Jr.
CMR 415 Box 8340
APO, AE 09114

www.AuthorChrisDavisJr.com

TO MY FAMILY,

THANK YOU FOR YOUR CONTINUED SUPPORT THROUGH THE JOURNEY OF WRITING & PUBLISHING THESE BOOKS. YOU ARE MY "WHY," AND I LOVE YOU TO THE MOON AND BACK!

MARY B. KENNER

INVENTED A BATHROOM TISSUE HOLDER
TO MAKE IT CONVENIENT

TO GET YOUR TOILET PAPER
FROM THE ROLL WHEN YOU NEED IT

SARAH BOONE

INVENTED THE IRONING BOARD FOR OUR CLOTHES TO BE PRESSED

SO THAT WE COULD LOOK OUR BEST WHEN WE GET DRESSED

CHRISTINA M. JENKINS

INVENTED THE SEW-IN WEAVE TECHNIQUE

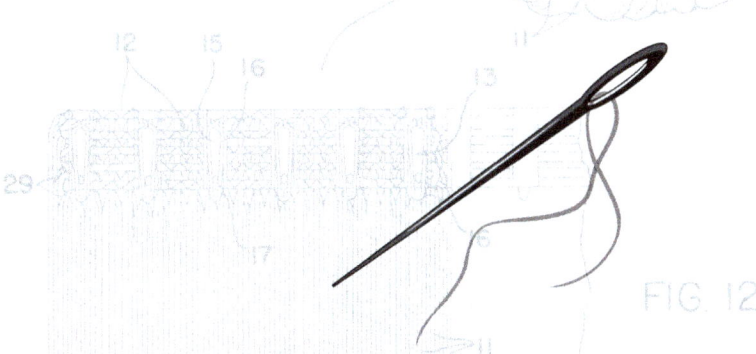

TO MAKE DIVERSE HAIRSTYLES
EASIER TO ACHIEVE

ANNA M. MANGIN

INVENTED THE **PASTRY FORK** TO MAKE DELICIOUS TREATS LIKE **PIES & COOKIES** AND OTHER KINDS OF SWEETS

MADAME C.J. WALKER

INVENTED PRODUCTS FOR BEAUTY AND NATURAL HAIR

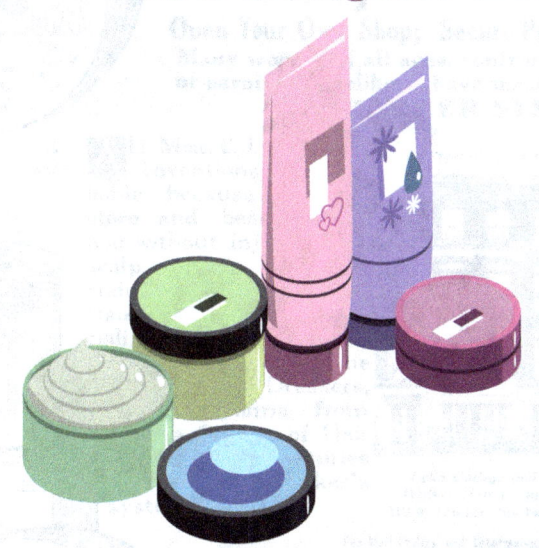

AND SOLD SO MANY THAT SHE BECOME A SELF-MADE MILLIONAIRE

SHIRLEY A. JACKSON

INVENTED THE TOUCH-TONE TELEPHONE

AND CALLER ID
SO THAT WE WOULD KNOW WHO'S CALLING OUR HOMES

SARAH E. GOODE

INVENTED A BED THAT FOLDED INTO A DESK

SO THAT AFTER YOU FINISHED WORKING, YOU COULD GET SOME REST

INVENTED A HOME SECURITY SYSTEM

THAT WE COULD MONITOR FROM OUR TELEVISIONS

LYDA D. NEWMAN

INVENTED A **BRUSH THAT WAS EASY TO CLEAN**

TO IMPROVE ON **EFFICIENCY & HYGIENE**

RUANE S. JETER

INVENTED A TOASTER
THAT YOU COULD SET

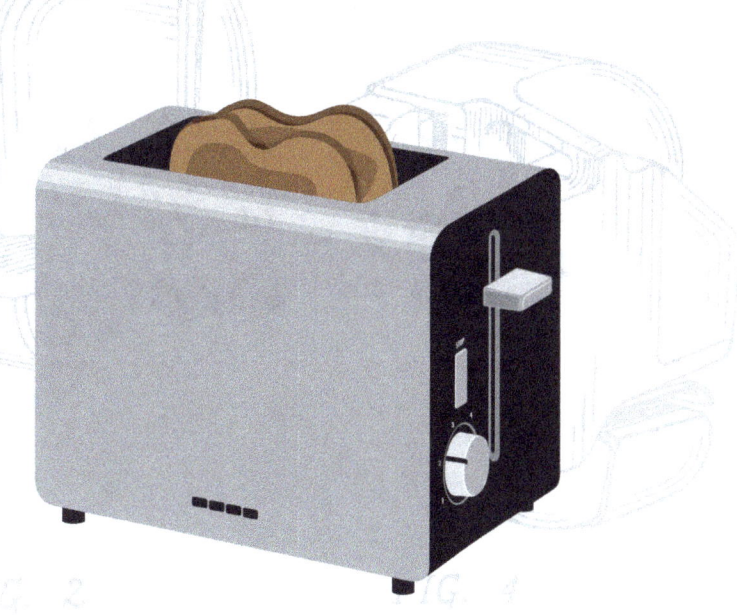

TO POP UP AUTOMATICALY
WHEN YOUR TOAST IS AS BROWN AS YOU'D WANT IT TO GET

WE'VE ONLY SCRATCH THE SURFACE OF WHAT YOU CAN ACHIEVE

IF YOU DO WHAT IT TAKES TO FOLLOW YOUR DREAMS!

CHRISTOPHER DAVIS, JR.

WROTE THIS BOOK TO TEACH YOU ABOUT INVENTIONS

Christopher is the owner of Lawn Ninja Residential Lawn Care, LLC. When not contributing to making the world a greener place, he focuses on his mission to educate, inspire and empower his community. This book is near and dear to his heart—and he hopes you'll love it too! Christopher is originally from Columbia, South Carolina, but currently resides in Germany.

SRI SAYEKTI, FAHIM PRANTO AND PRATAP SHARMA

ILLUSTRATED THIS BOOK TO CAPTURE YOUR ATTENTION

www.ingramcontent.com/pod-product-compliance
Lightning Source LLC
Chambersburg PA
CBHW071418290426
44108CB00014B/1884